TRACES OF THE ANN ARBOR RAILROAD

D. C. JESSE BURKHARDT

AMERICA
THROUGH
TIME

*To Renae, for sharing the peaceful summer magic of riding
bikes along the Betsie Valley Trail from Frankfort to Beulah;
and for the mystery of the sunset breezes on July 27, 2020*

America Through Time
An imprint of Sutton Publishing Inc
www.through-time.com
office@through-time.com

First published 2021
Reprinted 2025

ISBN 978-1-63499-297-8

Typeset in Sabon LT Std
Printed and bound in the United States of America

All photographs by D. C. Jesse Burkhardt, except where otherwise indicated.

CONTENTS

ACKNOWLEDGMENTS

I want to express sincere thanks to the following individuals and organizations for their valuable contributions to *Traces of the Ann Arbor Railroad*: Alan Sutton of Fonthill Media, with appreciation for believing in the project and all the support; Kena Longabaugh, Fonthill Media managing editor, for expert editorial work and assistance; Dennis Schmidt, for sharing many wonderful photos of Michigan railroad scenes over the years; Peter Hayes, for providing several sweet shots of the AA; Drayton Blackgrove, for photos and for the Jackson-area roots; Kristian Foondle, Michigan Department of Transportation Rail Program Specialist, for photos, info, and the shared affection for the Double A; Harriet Miller, for the photo in the heart of the fading Elberta yard; Jeff Ruetsche of Arcadia Publishing, for support and publishing advice in the early stages of "Traces"; Tom Lacinski, Scott Sparling, and Larry Moon Yaek, for photos and for sharing times in the 1970s on the AARR and its car ferries; Eric Wagner, for the clever coffee cup quip; Ryan Katon, for the photo of the AA southbound crossing the Huron River; Robert Warrick, for informative responses to several questions; Grover and Ruth Sparling, for inviting me on that first trip to Frankfort in 1969; Pro Photo Supply of Portland, Oregon, for top quality prints from my collection of archival slides; James Chapman of Gorge Ink, White Salmon, Washington, for expertise, technical assistance, and photo scans; Rick George, for support and encouragement of my work; Bryce Dreeszen, treasurer of Friends of the Betsie Valley Trail; the Ann Arbor Railroad Facebook site and all of its enthusiastic, informative members; Fred Eaglesmith, for writing the engaging song "Freight Train"; Mom and Dad, always, for love and support and our Michigan heritage; Renae Cannon and Clare Burkhardt, for home fires, love, and family.

One final note: The organization known as "Friends of the Betsie Valley Trail" has been instrumental in helping to preserve the old Ann Arbor Railroad route between Frankfort and Thompsonville as a recreational corridor. The trail honors and preserves the memory and historic importance of the Ann Arbor to the region, and to demonstrate my appreciation for the group's work, I intend to donate a portion of the proceeds from sales of this book to assist efforts to maintain and enhance the corridor.

INTRODUCTION

And every time I slip behind
Even further back
I wish some switchman would come out of the fog
And change my track.

Fred Eaglesmith, "Freight Train," Bash Music (ASCAP)

Fifteen years ago, Arcadia Publishing published *Images of Rail: The Ann Arbor Railroad*. It was my first book in honor of the Ann Arbor, the tracks of which served Michigan and Ohio, while its car ferries directly interchanged with several railroads across Lake Michigan in four different cities. The book delved into the history of the AA and its enchanting car ferry fleet, from its origins in the 1890s virtually all the way up to the book's publication in 2005.

Now it is 2020, and Fonthill Media has graciously agreed to publish a new book that celebrates and updates the life and heritage of this unique and intriguing railroad. *Traces of the Ann Arbor Railroad* tracks the carrier's historic "footprints," with a collection of photographs, maps, and other materials that reflect the many changes over recent decades. The primary focus of this book begins in the 1960s, an era of dramatic evolution for the company. This was the time when the Wabash Railroad, which then controlled the Ann Arbor, exited the scene in 1963 and the Detroit, Toledo & Ironton roared in to take over.

Traces of the Ann Arbor Railroad is not intended to be an exhaustive review of the "nuts and bolts" of the Ann Arbor's operations, but rather a reflective and appreciative overview. The photographs and narrative within these ninety-six pages chronicle the profound impact the "Annie" had on those who witnessed the railroad in action, particularly during the decades the AA car ferries steamed out of Frankfort Harbor and across Lake Michigan, loaded with freight cars. Indeed, the fact that so many people remain fascinated with this railroad company is a strong tribute to its importance.

The word "Traces" in the title effectively captures what is presented in this book. *Webster's New Collegiate Dictionary* defines traces as: "A mark or line left by something that has passed … to follow the footprints, track, or trail of." With this concept as a focus, on some pages there will be photographs of the same location seen in different years or even different decades, serving essentially as a "time machine" to spotlight the transition that has taken place.

The Ann Arbor Railroad first caught my attention in 1969. I was fifteen at the time, and living in Jackson, Michigan, about forty miles due west of Ann Arbor, the railroad's namesake city. That year, the parents of one of my closest friends invited me to come along for a few days vacationing in Frankfort, Michigan, a small resort town on Lake Michigan in the northwest corner of the state. I had never been to Frankfort and knew nothing about the area.

Arriving in Frankfort on a summer day in 1969, I was impressed and intrigued to see several reddish-orange locomotives, a large freight yard, and a huge car ferry being loaded with freight cars, all right there in the adjacent community of Elberta, across what I soon learned was Betsie Bay. The locale—the beach, the waves, the quaint town, and perhaps most of all the trains and car ferries—hooked me hard.

A short stub of road called Sac Street led directly to the beach, and I followed it. "I sat with my back against the lighthouse on the Frankfort Harbor breakwater for a long time, enjoying the July breezes and the sound of the Lake Michigan waves. A trio of Ann Arbor road engines hummed at me from across Betsie Bay," I wrote in a journal I maintained at the time.

I found out that Frankfort—or more precisely Elberta, where the car ferry docks were located—was the northern terminus of the Ann Arbor Railroad. Its southern terminus was in Toledo, Ohio, nearly 300 miles away. Freight trains were constantly in transit with cars that had been unloaded from, or were soon to be loaded into, the big car ferries, which at that time were headed to either Manitowoc or Kewaunee, port cities in Wisconsin on Lake Michigan's western shore, or to Menominee, in the Upper Peninsula of Michigan. A fourth destination to Manistique, Michigan, where the AA connected with its subsidiary Manistique & Lake Superior Railroad, had been abandoned just one year earlier.

Over several summers, Frankfort and the Ann Arbor Railroad became a travel destination. Sometimes I camped at the Betsie River Campground, near AA milepost 289, about three miles out of town. I had a blue 1966 Corvair and a sleeping bag, and that was it—no tent and no frills. I simply tossed the sleeping bag out on the grass next to my car and savored the Michigan summer. The campsites there were directly alongside the rail line heading to Elberta. There was not even a fence between the tracks and the tent sites.

Invariably, there would be at least one freight train "visiting" while I was sacked out in my sleeping bag during the dark night of crickets and fireflies, and I wrote about the magic of that experience in my journal:

A few miles out of Frankfort was the Betsie River Campground. Now and then I'd sleep there under the endless stars, a few feet from the mainline of the Ann Arbor Railroad. One long train usually passed through in the night, heading in to Boat Landing Yard; its baritone air horn sounding in the distance would wake me, then soon the train would come hissing and clanking and squealing out of the darkness, and I'd sit up and watch until the faint lights of the caboose passed by, disappearing into the trees …

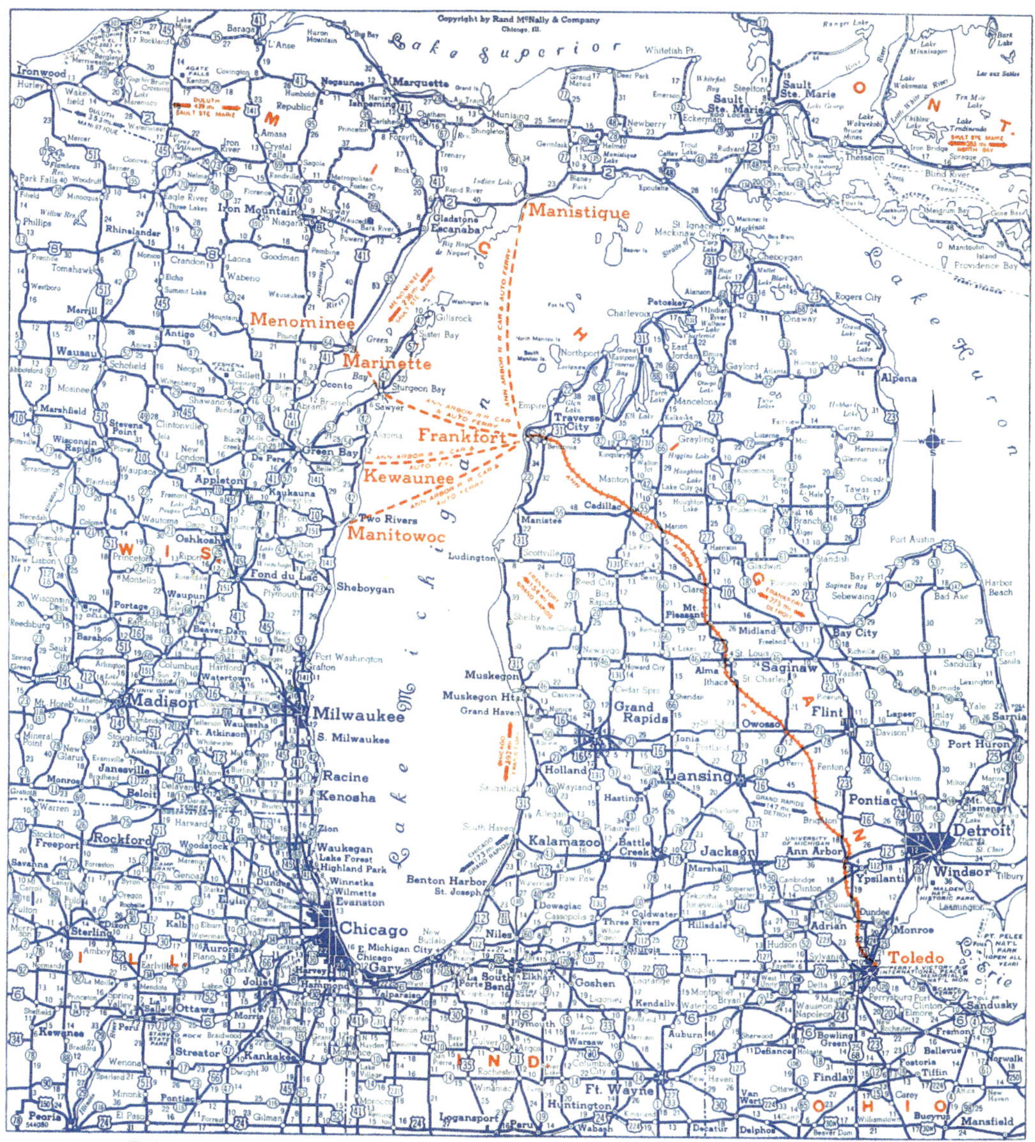

BY LAND AND WATER: The Ann Arbor Railroad cut diagonally across the state of Michigan, running northwest from Toledo, Ohio, to Elberta and Frankfort on the shore of Lake Michigan. From there, AA car ferries went in four additional directions: to Manitowoc and Kewaunee in Wisconsin, and to Menominee and Manistique in Michigan's Upper Peninsula. [*Author's collection*]

First launched in 1892, the AA's car ferries out of Elberta served four separate ports at the peak of operations: two in Wisconsin and two in Michigan's Upper Peninsula. Beginning in the late 1960s, the number of destinations succumbed one by one to market forces over which the railroad had little control.

The car ferries were traditionally geared to serve as a Chicago bypass, because Chicago's congested rail network was regarded as a freight bottleneck. But in the 1960s and 1970s, with trends toward longer trains and larger freight cars, the operating efficiency of the car ferries was being reduced. Each ferry carried about twenty-four to thirty cars; thus, a train with seventy-five cars would require three ferry trips to be moved across the lake—and larger freight cars meant fewer cars could be moved per trip. The AA ferry with the largest capacity was the 366-foot *Wabash*, built in 1927 and later renamed *City of Green Bay*. It had a listed capacity of thirty-two cars, but again, the size of each car would be a big factor in those calculations.

Yet perhaps the biggest drawback leading to the demise of the Lake Michigan car ferry network was a basic one: labor costs. Naturally, moving traffic across the lake via the ferries required boat crews in addition to railroad crews. However, the car ferries generally had crews of thirty to forty; in essence, that represented one employee—or more—per freight car. At some point, given these realities, routing trains through Chicago instead of across Lake Michigan no longer seemed like such a daunting or inefficient prospect.

Changes since the end of the decade of DT&I ownership in the mid-1970s almost need a program to keep up with. Here are the basics: On April 1, 1976, the state of Michigan contracted with Conrail to operate the entire AA system on an interim basis. In 1977, the state purchased the Ann Arbor Railroad to preserve the route, which faced abandonment. On October 1, 1977, Michigan Interstate Railway Company was created to take over all "Ann Arbor Railroad System" operations, including the car ferries. In 1980, Detroit-based Grand Trunk Western acquired the DT&I. In April 1982, Michigan Interstate cited insufficient funding to continue and withdrew to covering only the forty-five miles between Ann Arbor and Toledo, under the name Ann Arbor Railroad. With no rail carrier to serve Elberta, car ferry service came to an abrupt halt.

In October 1982, a new carrier, Michigan Northern Railway, took over freight service between Alma and Frankfort, but the car ferries were no more. In the same month, the Tuscola & Saginaw Bay expanded to take on the former AA route between Ann Arbor and Alma. In May 1984, Tuscola & Saginaw Bay's reach grew larger as the state booted Michigan Northern and instead selected T&SB to handle all rail operations between Ann Arbor and Frankfort. In the mid-1980s, the tracks from Frankfort to Yuma were taken out of service and later abandoned. Finally, in March 2006, the Great Lakes Central took over all business on the ex-AA territory from Yuma to Ann Arbor, as well as several other rail lines into northern Michigan. And that's where the map stands as of September 2020.

It has now been nearly forty years since the last AA car ferry sailed from Elberta on its way to Wisconsin in April 1982, and the long freight trains that fed the comings and goings of the steamship fleet have stopped traveling the line. Yet all these years later, the Ann Arbor Railroad still exists, albeit under fresh ownership and now as a shortline.

The "new" Ann Arbor Railroad operates from its origination yard in Toledo to Osmer (at milepost 50.5 on the original Ann Arbor Railroad mainline), where there is a small interchange yard about six miles north of the city of Ann Arbor. From Osmer, the Great Lakes Central—a regional carrier created in 2006—provides service to the north along what previously was AA territory. GLC moves freight on the former AA route all the way to Cadillac (at milepost 226.9). Thus, of the AA's 292-mile route between Toledo (milepost 0.0) and the ferry docks at Elberta, roughly 227 miles of track are still in use moving freight in 2020.

Beyond Cadillac, ex-AA rails are still in place another twenty-one miles to a station called Yuma (milepost 248.0), where foundry sand was mined for many years. However, the sand pits closed in 2015. The Cadillac-Yuma segment is currently out of service, but the rails remain in place. As of 2020, the trackage from Yuma to Elberta (milepost 291.8) and Frankfort (milepost 292.0), about forty-four miles, is the only part of the Ann Arbor's core Toledo-Frankfort route where the tracks have been removed.

Yet there is consolation in a very positive development related to the abandonment of the 22-mile segment between Frankfort and Thompsonville. In 1999, the Michigan Department of Natural Resources—which acquired the former AA railroad corridor between Elberta-Frankfort and Thompsonville in 1988—signed an agreement with the Betsie Valley Trail Management Council to develop a "rails-to-trails" biking and pedestrian pathway linking Thompsonville with Elberta and Frankfort. The scenic trail officially opened to the public in 2005.

With *Traces of the Ann Arbor Railroad,* my objective is to provide a creative and affectionate look back at the railroad and describe how different sections of it have been transformed over the past several decades. In these pages, I also want to honor the company's many employees, in whatever capacity they served.

The heritage of this company is still dearly missed by so many of us who were there to observe the railroad's activities and experience a journey across Lake Michigan on one of the car ferries. And indeed, seeing freight cars being pushed onto the tracks that lined the car deck, with the big boat creaking and listing slightly to one side or the other with the weight, will always be unforgettable.

White Salmon, Washington
September 16, 2020

 For a high school kid with an affection for railroads, discovering Frankfort in 1969—a town with majestic scenery as well as freight trains coming and going—was truly striking.

1

NEW CONNECTIONS:
THE DETROIT, TOLEDO & IRONTON DECADE,
1963-1973

In addition to being a charming and uncrowded community with a lovely beach on the shore of Lake Michigan, Frankfort was an important transportation center; a coastal city with economic purpose. Trains came all the way from Toledo, Ohio, to feed the Ann Arbor Railroad's fleet of car ferries.

D. C. Jesse Burkhardt, journal entry, July 2, 1971

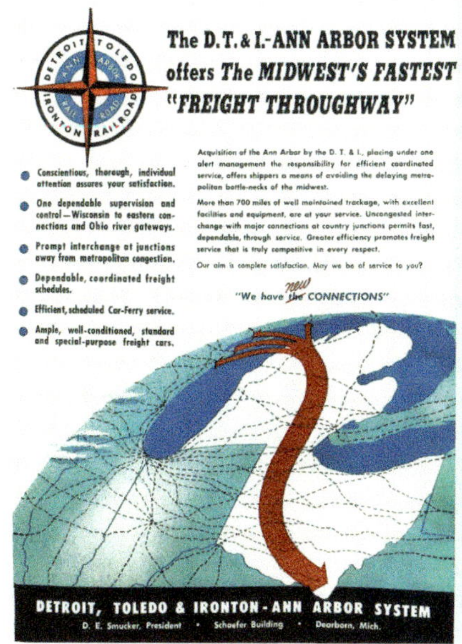

FRESH CONNECTION: The Detroit, Toledo & Ironton Railroad purchased the Ann Arbor in 1963, creating a seamless transportation network that ran from southern Ohio to northwestern Michigan, with the car ferry fleet taking freight cars across Lake Michigan to four additional cities. This advertisement highlighted the benefits of the combined system. [*Author's collection*]

FIVE IN THE HARBOR: The docks at Elberta, Michigan, were often bustling with activity during the nine decades (1892-1982) the Ann Arbor Railroad operated its cross-lake car ferries, but the level of activity in this 1930s-era scene is impressive. Five car ferries are in the harbor, being loaded or unloaded or waiting for their turn. Left to right are: *Wabash, Ann Arbor #7, Ann Arbor #5, Ann Arbor #3,* and *Ann Arbor #6.* The railroad launched a total of eight car ferries, and by the time this photo was taken, *Ann Arbor #1* and *Ann Arbor #2* were already retired. *Ann Arbor #4* was retired in 1937, so it's possible the entire active fleet was in the harbor at this moment. [*Collection of Larry Moon Yaek*]

OPPOSITE PAGE:

TRAFFIC TEAM (ABOVE): The Ann Arbor's twenty-strong Traffic Department attended a company meeting in Chicago in January 1939 and took time to pose for this group photograph. For several decades—from 1925 to 1963—the Ann Arbor was a subsidiary of Wabash Railroad and enjoyed a period of great stability. But these men didn't know that the world was about to be altered forever: Less than eight months after this event in Chicago, Germany invaded Poland and effectively ignited World War II. [*Author's collection*]

CHANGING TECHNOLOGY (BELOW): Following the war, technological advancements accelerated. By the early 1950s, the Ann Arbor's steam locomotives—such as #2481, built in 1923 and scrapped in 1951—were being replaced by new diesel units. [*Author's collection*]

ANN ARBOR RAILROAD TRAFFIC DEPT.
STAFF MEETING
JANUARY 9, 1939   CHICAGO, ILLINOIS

A DECADE REMAINING (LEFT):
Ann Arbor #52 rests on a gritty service track in Toledo, Ohio, on September 2, 1953, as it awaits its next run to Elberta. The AA purchased fourteen of these Alco diesels new in 1950, and just more than ten years after this photo was taken, all of them were replaced by ten General Motors Electro-Motive Division GP35s when Detroit, Toledo & Ironton obtained the AA from Wabash Railroad. [*Photo by G. E. Lloyd*]

RETURN TO YUMA (BELOW): A covered hopper assigned to move sand from the mining pits at Yuma, Michigan, is parked outside the AA's locomotive shops in Owosso, Michigan (AA milepost 106.0). Most of the sand was used to make casting molds for automobile engines manufactured in Ohio. The Yuma mines closed in 2015. [*Photo by Dennis Schmidt*]

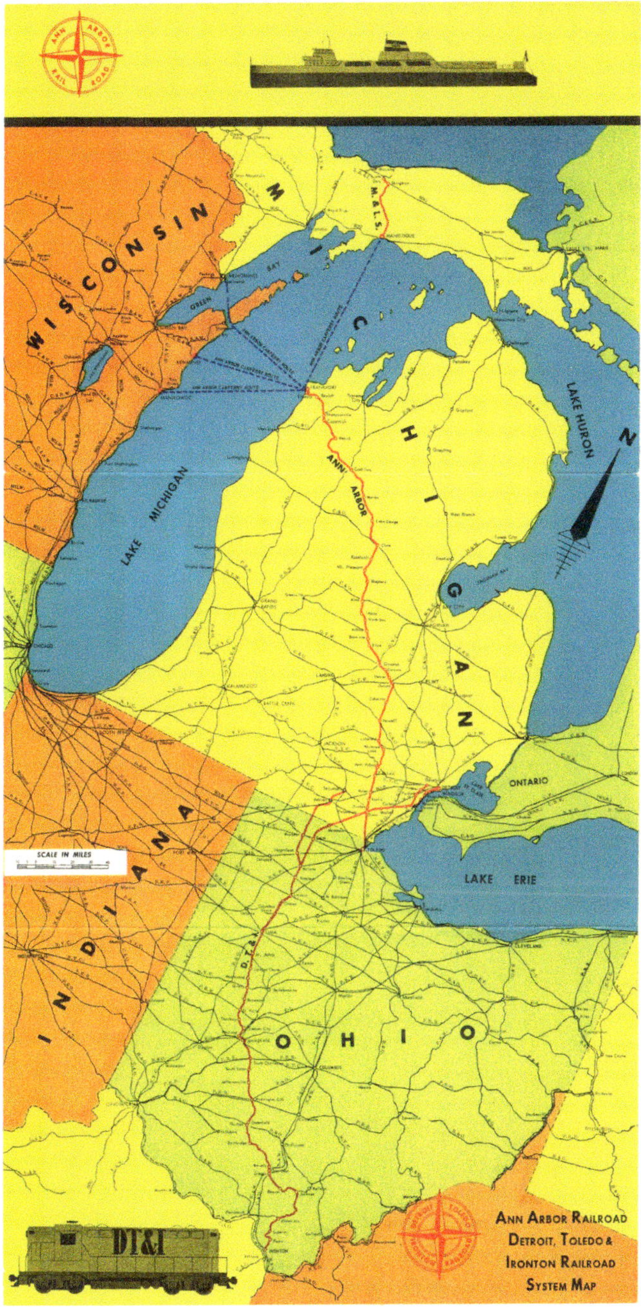

EXPANSION MODE: After the Detroit, Toledo & Ironton purchased the Ann Arbor, it swiftly proceeded to promote the new rail network. This colorful map from 1964 highlights the consolidated routes of the two rail companies in bright red. It seemed to be a perfect Midwestern marriage, with DT&I cutting north-south across virtually the entire length of Ohio and the AA doing the same across Michigan. Sadly, the marriage lasted only ten years, coming apart in 1973. [*Author's collection*]

BLASTING OUT OF FLAT ROCK: Ann Arbor GP35 #386 powers a long freight out of a siding near DT&I's big yard complex at Flat Rock, Michigan, in April 1969. Note the black number boards on the locomotive. These were difficult to read, and the configuration was later changed to a white background with black numbers. [*Photographer unknown; author's collection*]

LETTERHEAD CONNECTION: In 1963, the DT&I and the Ann Arbor joined up and started moving trains as a team. To make it official, the railroad created appealing new corporate letterhead featuring the wonderful slogan, "We Have the Connections." [*Author's collection*]

A LONG WAY FROM HOME: DT&I GP35 #355 and AA GP35 #386 take a break on a yard track in Cincinnati, Ohio, in October 1968. DT&I had trackage rights into the city, and the railroad sent its AA units wherever the company decided it needed them. [*Photographer unknown; author's collection*]

SOMEWHERE UP NORTH: A long-haul freight on the Ann Arbor mainline rolls through a crisp November day at an unidentified location in northern Michigan. Three of the railroad's signature GP35s power the train, with #389 in the lead. [*Photographer unknown; author's collection*]

THE COMPASS LOGO: When the Detroit, Toledo & Ironton took over the Ann Arbor, the AA's logo was switched from the Wabash-styled flag to the DT&I's compass design. The photo above shows the new imagery on the side of a freshly painted caboose. Years later, a weathered, deteriorating logo on the closed yard office in Ann Arbor, Michigan (below), is a stark reminder of the railroad's history of ownership by the DT&I, which unfortunately culminated in the AA's bankruptcy in 1973.

ANOTHER CLASSIC DESIGN: The Great Northern Railway's iconic Rocky Mountain goat was often seen on trains rolling through Michigan during the years the DT&I owned the Ann Arbor. The GN goat and the DT&I compass were arguably among the most memorable logos in the history of American railroads.

TOLEDO TRIO: AA #386 leads two other GP35s on a mixed freight moving through Toledo. Three locomotives were typical on long-haul trains in transit between Toledo and Elberta during the decade the DT&I was in charge of operations along the line. [*Photographer unknown; author's collection*]

SCRAP LINE: A long line of DT&I boxcars stand quietly on yard tracks at Cadillac, Michigan, in 1997. The cars seem destined for scrapping, as a white line crosses out the road number on each car—a sure sign the owner no longer sees a future for them.

ESSENTIAL ANN ARBOR: In July 1975, a long southbound train is ready to pull out of Elberta's Boat Landing Yard as it begins the 292-mile journey to Toledo with freight off the car ferries from Wisconsin. Note the obsolete "tell-tales" above the engines; these were designed to alert trainmen atop the freight cars of structures ahead with low overhead clearance. [*Photographer unknown; author's collection*]

FRESH OFF THE BOAT: A long "FT" (Frankfort to Toledo) train heads southeast through Alma, Michigan, in May 1975, just two years before the state of Michigan purchased the entire Ann Arbor route to preserve rail service in the corridor. Note the trio of yellow Green Bay & Western boxcars behind the engines. Wisconsin-based GB&W was a faithful and essential interchange partner for the AA right until the end of car ferry service in April 1982. [*Photo by Dennis Schmidt*]

WARNING: In July 2014, probably five or six decades after this wooden "Close Clearance" sign was placed alongside a spur track on the Ann Arbor north of Owosso, the wording is still plainly legible—a silent tribute to the sign-makers of their era.

OPTIONS AT OWOSSO: In 2014, a fading station sign on Grand Trunk Western's long-closed passenger depot at Owosso displays distances to cities once served by GTW: Owosso to Grand Haven, 109.79 miles; Owosso to Detroit, 78.52 miles. Travelers in Owosso could also board passenger trains operated by the New York Central and the Ann Arbor. The Ann Arbor ended its passenger service in 1950.

ANN ARBOR TRANSFORMATION: Ferry Yard in Ann Arbor (milepost 44.4) was a busy place in the 1970s, as reflected in this scene (above) from May 21, 1976. The shiny yard tracks are filled with a variety of freight cars and a local switcher is stationed at the yard. Jump ahead thirty years, however, to June 2006 (below), and the situation is quite different. The yard tracks are long gone, buried in vegetation, and the yard office has been boarded up. The mainline and a rarely used siding are all that remain. [*Top photo by Dennis Schmidt*]

HEED THE TIMETABLE: Boxcars have come off the rails while shuffling cars in Elberta in July 1971. Fortunately, this relatively minor mishap occurred in the yard and not inside a car ferry or on the loading apron. A rule displayed in the Ann Arbor's October 1964 timetable (below) specifically detailed how to ward off this type of problem. In short: reduce the speed of switching operations.

AVOID DAMAGE—SWITCH CUSTOMERS CARS CAREFULLY

JUDGING SPEED

Accurate judgment of coupling speed depends upon correct timing. An excellent way to get accurate timing without a watch is to count "one hundred and thirty-one, one hundred and thirty-two" and so on as the car passes a stationary point. With a little practice counting can be done at the rate of one a second.

Ability to closely estimate speed at time car strikes is extremely important because impact force builds up as the square of the speed. This means that impact delivered by a car coupled at 8 mph is not four times that at 2 mph but 16 TIMES AS GREAT. Damage to freight and car can be avoided by always keeping coupling speed within the safe range—NOT OVER 4 MILES PER HOUR—A BRISK WALK.

Impact Force At Various Striking Speeds

	Car Coupled at	Units of De-struction
Safe	1 mph	1
	2 "	4
	3 "	9
	4 "	16
Damaging	5 "	25
	6 "	36
	7 "	49
	8 "	64
	9 "	81
	10 "	100

To Find Coupling Speed of 40 Foot and 50 Foot Cars

Sight vertical end of car body on a fixed point and note the number of seconds it takes car to pass. Speed in miles per hour is shown opposite.

Damage as a result of Rough Handling makes up a large part of the claim bill for Loss and Damage to Freight. From the Railroad standpoint it is the major item in the expense. We all know that Rough Handling can be reduced, often eliminated. It is hoped that this table will be helpful in your efforts to prevent Rough Handling.

Switch crews must function as a team. Clear signals properly given are mighty important; talk it over . . . Prevent Rough Handling . . . it can be done.

Seconds	40 Foot Car Miles Per Hour	50 Foot Car Miles Per Hour
1	28	35
2	14	17.5
3	9.3	11.6
4	7	8.7
5	5.6	7
6	4.7	5.9
7	4	5
8	3.5	4.4
9	3.1	3.9
10	2.8	3.5
11	2.5	3.1
12	2.3	2.9
13	2.15	2.7
14	2	2.5

2

END OF THE ANN ARBOR CAR FERRIES

We got a last ride at dusk from the Highway 31-Highway 115 junction in Benzonia, and as we hit the outskirts of Elberta, the car ferry Viking sounded its half-hour warning horn. Once again we were cutting it too tight. But we got aboard and at last headed westbound with the moon bright. We slept on the deck through the cold sailing night, and when we awoke we were pulling into the Kewaunee harbor.

D. C. Jesse Burkhardt, journal entry, August 30, 1977

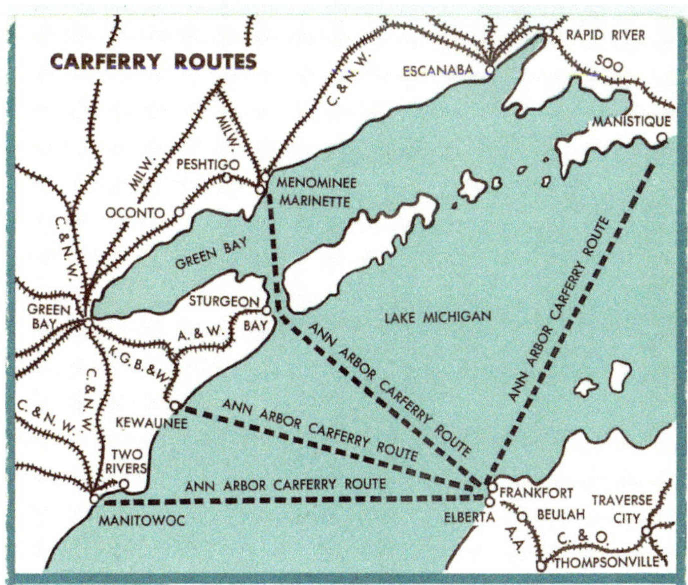

FOUR DIRECTIONS: Car ferries once sailed to four destinations out of Elberta, ironically matching the four points of the compass logo the AA used during the decade of Detroit, Toledo & Ironton ownership that began in 1963. [*Author's collection*]

FOGG AT BOAT LANDING: To promote its manufacturing prowess, the American Locomotive Company (Alco) contracted with famed artist Howard Fogg in the 1940s to create a series of paintings of new Alco locomotives in the paint schemes of the railroads that placed the orders. One of Fogg's nearly fifty iconic watercolors resulting from the marketing campaign featured Ann Arbor #51 and a sister unit switching freight cars at Boat Landing Yard in Elberta, with two car ferries steaming in the distance. [*Author's collection*]

OPPOSITE PAGE:

MINERAL SPRINGS (ABOVE): Frankfort's mineral water fountain, a tourist attraction in a city park, is featured in this century-old postcard postmarked in South Frankfort on June 20, 1910. In 1911, South Frankfort was renamed "Elberta" in honor of the tasty peaches that grew locally. The tracks in the background were part of the Ann Arbor's branch into downtown Frankfort, a portion of which remained in use until the mid-1980s. [*Author's collection*]

COAL TO OIL (BELOW): The car ferry *Wabash* pours out coal smoke as it steams out of Elberta in an image from a postcard mailed in 1959. *Wabash*, launched in Toledo in 1927, was the eighth and last new car ferry constructed for the AA. In 1962, *Wabash* was rebuilt; at that time, it was converted from coal-fired to oil-fired and renamed *City of Green Bay*. [*Author's collection*]

DOCKING AT MENOMINEE: An undated postcard shows the Ann Arbor's ferry slip at Menominee, Michigan, probably in the late 1940s judging by the automobiles in the scene. Service to Menominee ended in 1970; it was the second of the AA's four cross-lake routes to be dropped when the railroad sought to cut costs as traffic declined. [*Author's collection*]

SMOKING IN MANITOWOC: In this 1950s postcard scene, a Chesapeake & Ohio car ferry slowly makes its way east out of the harbor at Manitowoc, Wisconsin, on its way to Ludington, Michigan, home to the C&O's car ferry fleet. Plowing through the waves right ahead of the C&O ferry is an AA boat, smoking it up as it heads toward Elberta. [*Collection of Larry Moon Yaek*]

WESTBOUND BLUE: The Ann Arbor car ferry *Arthur K. Atkinson* (above), rebuilt from *Ann Arbor #6* in 1959 and renamed for a president of the Wabash Railroad, leaves Elberta and plows westward over the deep blue water of Lake Michigan on a run to Wisconsin in August 1970. In the photo below, an unidentified car ferry obscured by fog has just left Frankfort Harbor. By the summer of 1970, the ferry operation was down to just two routes—to Kewaunee and Manitowoc in Wisconsin.

SOUTHBOUND STANDBY: Four GP35s, all sporting new coats of paint, idle in Boat Landing Yard in the summer of 1979. Three are likely waiting to haul the next "FT" (Frankfort to Toledo) train, while the disconnected unit is probably power for the Elberta-Cadillac local. [*Photographer unknown; author's collection*]

NO COMPASS: A "Boat Train" rolls through Alma on October 21, 1978. Note how the attractive compass logo of former Ann Arbor owner DT&I has been painted over on two of the three locomotives seen here, reflecting the breakup between the two companies in the aftermath of the AA declaring bankruptcy in October 1973. [*Photo by Dennis Schmidt*]

NIGHT MOVES: After interchanging cars with the Green Bay & Western, the Ann Arbor car ferry *Viking*, loaded to the brim with boxcars, is ready to depart Kewaunee on another of its back and forth journeys across Lake Michigan. *Viking*, previously *Ann Arbor #7*, was rebuilt and renamed in 1965. [*Author's collection*]

ENDLESS SAND: Provided it was not nighttime or conditions were not too foggy, travelers going east on the car ferries would see this beautiful view of the high sand bluffs north of Frankfort as they neared the docks at Elberta. The magnificent Lake Michigan scenery was yet another level to the allure of the big ferry boats.

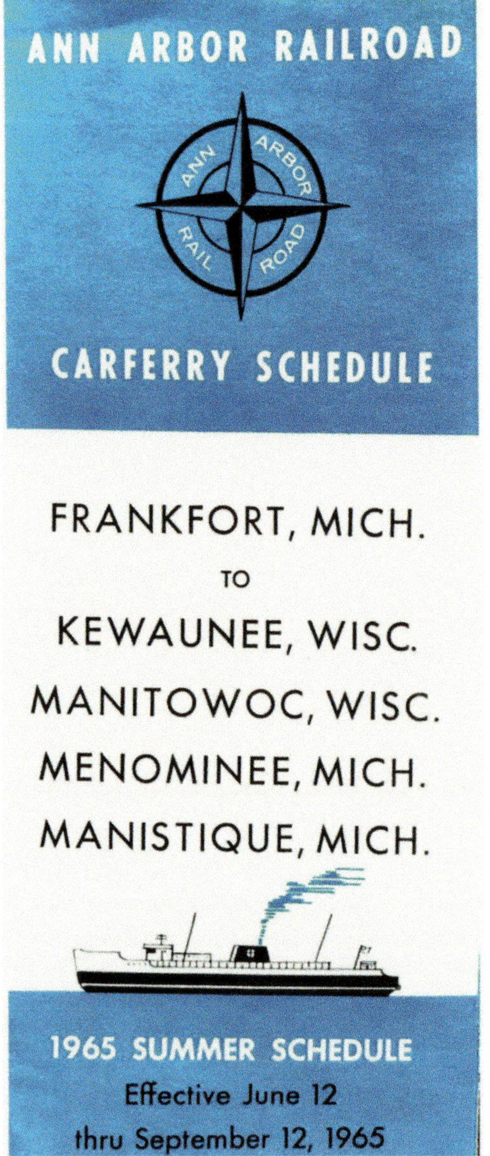

SUMMER SAILINGS: Between 1965 and 1971, the Ann Arbor slashed its ferry service by half, dropping its two runs to Michigan's Upper Peninsula. Yet even in the wake of those cutbacks, strong marketing continued for the railroad's two remaining ports of call in Wisconsin, as the artistic front of the 1971 brochure demonstrates. [*Author's collection*]

OPPOSITE PAGE:

TOURIST DRAW: Postcards featuring the car ferries were popular over the years, and the selection was extensive. These cards from the 1970s depict operations in Elberta. Top: The car ferry *Viking*, which in its last year on the job sported an energetic red trim that previously was all white. Middle: *Viking* with four boxcars in the foreground; in 2020, none of the railroads represented by those boxcars still exist. Bottom: An aerial view of the freight yard and ferry docks. [*Author's collection*]

Auto & Rail Car Ferry

Photo: John Penrod

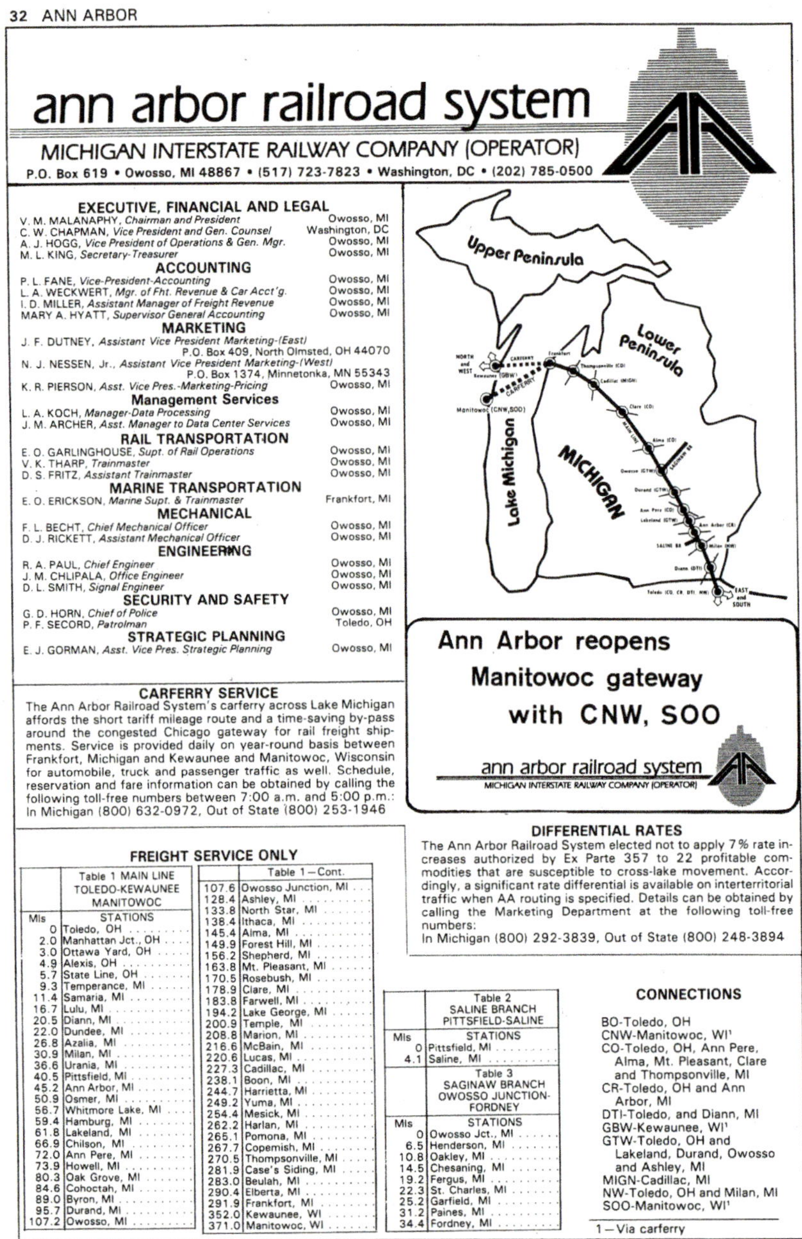

ann arbor railroad system

MICHIGAN INTERSTATE RAILWAY COMPANY (OPERATOR)

P.O. Box 619 • Owosso, MI 48867 • (517) 723-7823 • Washington, DC • (202) 785-0500

EXECUTIVE, FINANCIAL AND LEGAL

V. M. MALANAPHY, *Chairman and President*	Owosso, MI
C. W. CHAPMAN, *Vice President and Gen. Counsel*	Washington, DC
A. J. HOGG, *Vice President of Operations & Gen. Mgr.*	Owosso, MI
M. L. KING, *Secretary-Treasurer*	Owosso, MI

ACCOUNTING

P. L. FANE, *Vice-President-Accounting*	Owosso, MI
L. A. WECKWERT, *Mgr. of Fht. Revenue & Car Acct'g.*	Owosso, MI
I. D. MILLER, *Assistant Manager of Freight Revenue*	Owosso, MI
MARY A. HYATT, *Supervisor General Accounting*	Owosso, MI

MARKETING

J. F. DUTNEY, *Assistant Vice President Marketing-(East)*
P.O. Box 409, North Olmsted, OH 44070
N. J. NESSEN, Jr., *Assistant Vice President Marketing-(West)*
P.O. Box 1374, Minnetonka, MN 55343
K. R. PIERSON, *Asst. Vice Pres.-Marketing-Pricing*   Owosso, MI

Management Services

L. A. KOCH, *Manager-Data Processing*	Owosso, MI
J. M. ARCHER, *Asst. Manager to Data Center Services*	Owosso, MI

RAIL TRANSPORTATION

E. O. GARLINGHOUSE, *Supt. of Rail Operations*	Owosso, MI
V. K. THARP, *Trainmaster*	Owosso, MI
D. S. FRITZ, *Assistant Trainmaster*	Owosso, MI

MARINE TRANSPORTATION

E. O. ERICKSON, *Marine Supt. & Trainmaster*	Frankfort, MI

MECHANICAL

F. L. BECHT, *Chief Mechanical Officer*	Owosso, MI
D. J. RICKETT, *Assistant Mechanical Officer*	Owosso, MI

ENGINEERING

R. A. PAUL, *Chief Engineer*	Owosso, MI
J. M. CHLIPALA, *Office Engineer*	Owosso, MI
D. L. SMITH, *Signal Engineer*	Owosso, MI

SECURITY AND SAFETY

G. D. HORN, *Chief of Police*	Owosso, MI
P. F. SECORD, *Patrolman*	Toledo, OH

STRATEGIC PLANNING

E. J. GORMAN, *Asst. Vice Pres. Strategic Planning*	Owosso, MI

CARFERRY SERVICE

The Ann Arbor Railroad System's carferry across Lake Michigan affords the short tariff mileage route and a time-saving by-pass around the congested Chicago gateway for rail freight shipments. Service is provided daily on year-round basis between Frankfort, Michigan and Kewaunee and Manitowoc, Wisconsin for automobile, truck and passenger traffic as well. Schedule, reservation and fare information can be obtained by calling the following toll-free numbers between 7:00 a.m. and 5:00 p.m.: In Michigan (800) 632-0972, Out of State (800) 253-1946

Ann Arbor reopens Manitowoc gateway with CNW, SOO

ann arbor railroad system
MICHIGAN INTERSTATE RAILWAY COMPANY (OPERATOR)

DIFFERENTIAL RATES

The Ann Arbor Railroad System elected not to apply 7% rate increases authorized by Ex Parte 357 to 22 profitable commodities that are susceptible to cross-lake movement. Accordingly, a significant rate differential is available on interterritorial traffic when AA routing is specified. Details can be obtained by calling the Marketing Department at the following toll-free numbers:
In Michigan (800) 292-3839, Out of State (800) 248-3894

FREIGHT SERVICE ONLY

Mls	Table 1 MAIN LINE TOLEDO-KEWAUNEE MANITOWOC — STATIONS
0	Toledo, OH
2.0	Manhattan Jct., OH
3.0	Ottawa Yard, OH
4.9	Alexis, OH
5.7	State Line, OH
9.3	Temperance, MI
11.4	Samaria, MI
16.7	Lulu, MI
20.5	Diann, MI
22.0	Dundee, MI
26.8	Azalia, MI
30.9	Milan, MI
36.6	Urania, MI
40.5	Pittsfield, MI
45.2	Ann Arbor, MI
50.9	Osmer, MI
56.7	Whitmore Lake, MI
59.4	Hamburg, MI
61.8	Lakeland, MI
66.9	Chilson, MI
72.0	Ann Pere, MI
73.9	Howell, MI
80.3	Oak Grove, MI
84.6	Cohoctah, MI
89.0	Byron, MI
95.7	Durand, MI
107.2	Owosso, MI

Mls	Table 1 — Cont.
107.6	Owosso Junction, MI
128.4	Ashley, MI
133.8	North Star, MI
138.4	Ithaca, MI
145.4	Alma, MI
149.9	Forest Hill, MI
156.2	Shepherd, MI
163.8	Mt. Pleasant, MI
170.5	Rosebush, MI
178.9	Clare, MI
183.8	Farwell, MI
194.2	Lake George, MI
200.9	Temple, MI
208.8	Marion, MI
216.6	McBain, MI
220.6	Lucas, MI
227.3	Cadillac, MI
238.1	Boon, MI
244.7	Harrietta, MI
249.2	Yuma, MI
254.4	Mesick, MI
262.2	Harlan, MI
265.1	Pomona, MI
267.7	Copemish, MI
270.5	Thompsonville, MI
281.9	Case's Siding, MI
283.0	Beulah, MI
290.4	Elberta, MI
291.9	Frankfort, MI
352.0	Kewaunee, WI
371.0	Manitowoc, WI

Mls	Table 2 SALINE BRANCH PITTSFIELD-SALINE — STATIONS
0	Pittsfield, MI
4.1	Saline, MI

Mls	Table 3 SAGINAW BRANCH OWOSSO JUNCTION-FORDNEY — STATIONS
0	Owosso Jct., MI
6.5	Henderson, MI
10.8	Oakley, MI
14.5	Chesaning, MI
19.2	Fergus, MI
22.3	St. Charles, MI
25.2	Garfield, MI
31.2	Paines, MI
34.4	Fordney, MI

CONNECTIONS

BO-Toledo, OH
CNW-Manitowoc, WI[1]
CO-Toledo, OH, Ann Pere, Alma, Mt. Pleasant, Clare and Thompsonville, MI
CR-Toledo, OH and Ann Arbor, MI
DTI-Toledo, and Diann, MI
GBW-Kewaunee, WI[1]
GTW-Toledo, OH and Lakeland, Durand, Owosso and Ashley, MI
MIGN-Cadillac, MI
NW-Toledo, OH and Milan, MI
SOO-Manitowoc, WI[1]

1 — Via carferry

MANITOWOC REBIRTH: When a cracked crankshaft put the *Arthur K. Atkinson* out of service in 1973, the Ann Arbor was down to just one working car ferry, *Viking*. Because one boat could not effectively handle two destinations, the Kewaunee run was given priority and the route to Manitowoc was embargoed. Service to Manitowoc did not return for several years. The Michigan Interstate/Ann Arbor Railroad System listing in an early 1982 edition of the *Official Railway Guide* promoted the return of the route with an attention-grabbing "Ann Arbor reopens Manitowoc gateway" headline. The "success story" was short-lived, however, as all AA car ferry operations came to an end in April 1982. [*Author's collection*]

FORLORN: Ann Arbor single-door boxcar #1402 (above), a 40-foot car still in its Wabash-era look, rests in tall weeds at what's left of Boat Landing Yard in 1987. The once-common boxcars, with the "Direct Route Linking East-North-West" slogan and the flag logo that connected the AA with the "Follow the Flag" corporate branding of parent Wabash, were built by Pullman-Standard in Michigan City, Indiana, in the 1950s. The final freight train pulled out of Elberta with the last of the stored rolling stock in July 1988, but with the tracks leading to Ann Arbor boxcar #1325 (below) pulled up, this car missed the boat and was left high and dry in the deserted yard.

RUSTED OVER: It is the summer of 1988, and the rails of Boat Landing Yard (above), once bustling with long trains coming and going and freight cars being switched around, stand empty and rusted. No longer heard are the echoes of a ferry's steam whistle or the sound of steel wheels squealing along steel rails as ties creak under the weight. Within another year, the yard tracks will be gone, pushing this vital slice of Michigan history even further into the fog of memory. A mile down the tracks (bottom photo), the AA mainline—unused and forgotten—bends to the southeast as it leaves Elberta. [*Both photos by Scott Sparling*]

KEEP OFF: A fence stretches across the Ann Arbor mainline just northwest of the sand pits at Yuma in the late 1980s, marking the point beyond which trains would never again travel. Salvage crews were about to begin the sad process of tearing out the rails and ties from Yuma to Elberta and Frankfort. [*Photo by Ira Rosenberg*]

INTO THE LANDSCAPE: A billboard a few miles west of Clare, Michigan, invited tourists to head to Frankfort and take a ride on the Ann Arbor's car ferries, but as the years passed, the sign was forgotten. The photograph above was taken in October 1992, more than ten years after the AA's last ferry crossed Lake Michigan. The sign probably confused travelers who didn't know the status of ferry service. Fast forward to April 2005 (below), and the billboard is still there, although it has deteriorated further and trees have grown up around it. Why the obsolete advertisement was not removed, more than twenty years after ferry service stopped, remains a mystery.

AUTUMN MEMORIES: In October 1992, a decade after the car ferries halted operations, rails and ties of the Ann Arbor mainline are swallowed up by determined weeds near milepost 289, about three miles out of Elberta. From here, it was roughly one mile to the station called Junction Switch, where trains could be directed to either Elberta or Frankfort.

ROUNDHOUSE RUINS: For many decades, the roundhouse at Boat Landing Yard was a critical facility in the Ann Arbor's daily operations, but in this scene from June 2009, the discarded roundhouse is literally a shell of what it used to be. Its roof has collapsed, and its floor is overgrown with weeds and small trees. [*Photo by Scott Sparling*]

TURNTABLE TRANSITION: In August 1987, five years after the last car ferry left Elberta, Boat Landing Yard's disused turntable has been abandoned to the elements (above), with cattails growing in the turning pit and the control shanty falling apart from neglect. In the background, an idler flatcar—once a vital piece of equipment for loading and unloading the ferries—rusts alone among yard tracks obscured by a sea of weeds. In April 2005 (below), in a nod to Elberta's history, the turntable area has been cleaned up and blended into part of a waterfront park. [*Top photo by Scott Sparling*]

FERRY SUNSET: Twilight on a July evening in 1988 at Boat Landing Yard. In the distance is former Grand Trunk Railway car ferry *City of Milwaukee*, in a scene captured from atop one of the boxcars remaining in storage at the abandoned yard. The GT operated car ferries between Muskegon, Michigan, and Milwaukee, Wisconsin, until 1978. Soon after the GT ended service, *City of Milwaukee* was obtained by the state of Michigan for use by the Ann Arbor as it restarted limited service to Manitowoc. In 2000, the car ferry was towed to Manistee, Michigan, and turned into a floating museum. [*Photo by Scott Sparling*]

NOTICE TO PUBLIC
PROPOSAL F-8-633

Sale of Locomotives, Cabooses and Railroad Cars of the Former Ann Arbor Railroad and located in the Cadillac, Michigan, Owosso, Michigan and other areas along the former Ann Arbor Railroad line.

Sealed bids will be received on Tuesday, October 29, 1985, until 1 p.m., at the Michigan Department of Transportation, Right of Way Field office, 5463 Nixon Road, Dimondale, Michigan 48821, at which time and place all bids will be publicly opened and read for the sale and removal of former Ann Arbor Railroad Rolling Stock now owned by the Michigan Department of Transportation. Inspection arrangements at the various locations may be made on October 15, 16, and 17, 1985 by contacting John T. Mangan, at the Dimondale Field Office: Phone (517) 645-7621.

TO BE CONSIDERED ALL BIDS MUST BE ON THE PRESCRIBED BID PROPOSAL FORMS.

Specifications and Bid Proposal Forms may be obtained at the Michigan Department of Transportation, Right of Way Field Office, 5463 Nixon Road Dimondale, Michigan 48821; telephone number (517) 645-7621.

Rolling Stock located in the Owosso, Michigan area.

INSPECTION ARRANGEMENT MAY BE MADE BY CONTACTING: James W. Schell, Superintendent of Shops, 600 Oakwood Street, Owosso, Michigan 48867
Phone: (517) 723-5752

Item #	Car #	Car Type	Minimum Acceptable Bid	Amount of Bid
119	AA 10	Locomotive, Alco S-1 600 HP	$2,000.00	__________
120	AA 7	Locomotive, Alco S-1 600 HP	2,000.00	__________
121	AA 386	Locomotive, EMD 2500 HP	2,000.00	__________
122	AA 387	Locomotive, EMD 2500 HP	2,000.00	__________
123	AA 4636	40-Foot Boxcar	100.00	__________
124	AA 4629	40-Foot Boxcar	100.00	__________
125	AA 1326	40-Foot Boxcar	100.00	__________
126	AA 3395	Wrecking Flat for Car Trucks	100.00	__________
127	AA 4535	Flat-Pettibone Car	100.00	__________
128	AA 4510	Flatcar	100.00	__________
129	AA 35	Flatcar	100.00	__________
130	AA 4630	Ferry Idler	100.00	__________
131	AA 4516	Ferry Idler	100.00	__________
132	AA 4518	Flatcar	100.00	__________
133	AA 4505	Ferry Idler	100.00	__________
134	AA 5454	Gondola	100.00	__________
135	AA 4620	Cutdown 40-Foot Boxcar	100.00	__________
136	AA 2832	Caboose	100.00	__________
137	AA 4536	Flatcar	100.00	__________
138	AA 4646	40-Foot Boxcar	100.00	__________
139	AA 4635	40-Foot Boxcar	100.00	__________
140	AA 4632	40-Foot Boxcar	100.00	__________
141	AA 4626	40-Foot Boxcar	100.00	__________
142	AA 4625	40-Foot Boxcar	100.00	__________
143	AA 4634	40-Foot Boxcar	100.00	__________
144	AA 4645	40-Foot Boxcar	100.00	__________
145	AA 4623	40-Foot Boxcar	100.00	__________
146	AA 4622	40-Foot Boxcar	100.00	__________
147	AA 4624	40-Foot Boxcar	100.00	__________
148	AA 1276	40-Foot Boxcar	100.00	__________

RAILROAD FOR SALE: The state of Michigan purchased the Ann Arbor Railroad in 1977 to ward off its abandonment, but by the mid-1980s the state was cutting its losses on the failing carrier. In October 1985, the Michigan Department of Transportation ran newspaper ads for a public auction of surplus rolling stock, including freight cars, cabooses, and locomotives. For most items, a minimum bid of a mere $100 was required, but locomotives commanded an offer of at least $2,000. [*Author's collection*]

AUCTION ACTION: Upon hearing of the auction of AA equipment, Annie enthusiasts Tom Lacinski (left) and Scott Sparling held a mock celebration in Elberta based on their hoped-for purchase of a caboose. "Tom and I close the deal on his new caboose!" Sparling declared at the time—but their bid was ultimately unsuccessful. [*Photo by Harriet Miller*]

EXHAUSTED: Twenty years after this car ferry docking apron in Elberta was last used, its wood is rotting, its steel parts are rusting, and weeds have somehow taken root on it. It is July 15, 2002, and this decrepit loading slip—one of two that were in use here—is slowly collapsing into Betsie Bay.

LAST CALL: Boat Landing Yard is viewed from across Betsie Bay on July 11, 1988. In just ten days, this final cut of fifteen freight cars, in storage here for several years, will be hauled away from this once-extensive yard complex and rumble south on the rusty tracks out of town, closing the door on nearly a century of rail activity in the community. [*Photo by Scott Sparling*]

BRIDGE IN THE MIST: Rain soaks the autumn landscape and the deteriorating bridge over the Manistee River in this 1992 view looking northwest near Mesick, Michigan, ten years after daily service ended on this stretch of the AA route. The site is about halfway between Cadillac and Frankfort.

A BRIDGE NO LONGER: The muddy Manistee River quietly flows under what was once an active bridge that carried long freight trains on their way to and from the ferry slips at Elberta. The rails were pulled from the structure in the late 1990s. This haunting scene of what remains, shot from a drone, was captured in July 2018. [*Photo by Peter Hayes*]

3

TAKING OVER:

CONRAIL, MICHIGAN INTERSTATE, MICHIGAN NORTHERN, TUSCOLA & SAGINAW BAY, GREAT LAKES CENTRAL

Clare was where the east-west C&O (Chessie System) tracks crossed the north-south rails of the Ann Arbor. The two railroads interchanged freight cars in Clare, and the interchange track was active with seven cars waiting. I was hopeful a train would soon stop to collect them. After a while, a short C&O freight bounced over the AA diamond on its way to Saginaw. It didn't even slow down.

D. C. Jesse Burkhardt, journal entry, July 21, 1979

SKY BLUE DREAMS: In shiny fresh paint that matches the sky, Great Lakes Central GP38-2 #395 waits in Cadillac, Michigan, for its next task hauling freight.

CONRAIL BLUES: In 1977, the state of Michigan obtained the Ann Arbor from DT&I because transportation officials believed Conrail's 1976 consolidation plan for several bankrupt railroads would result in the loss of the "Double A Route." Ironically, as a stopgap to preserve service, Michigan contracted with Conrail to run the Ann Arbor, including the car ferries, from April 1976 until the end of September 1977.

NEW CARRIER, OLD EQUIPMENT: On October 1, 1977, newly formed Michigan Interstate Railway took over all operations on the Ann Arbor. New motive power was not part of the arrangement, however, as the yard switcher at Owosso in the summer of 1980 illustrates. Alco RS1 #21, its orange paint fading to pink, was built in 1950 but still on the job thirty years later. [*Photographer unknown; author's collection*]

FROM WISCONSIN WITH LOVE: Michigan Interstate/Ann Arbor Railroad System RS2 #301 (top), a former Green Bay & Western unit, switches covered hoppers in the snow in December 1979. The railroad purchased two of the ex-GB&W Alcos, #301 and #303, in 1979, when they were already nearly three decades old. Both locomotives were manufactured in 1950. Below, the same workhorse engine idles on the ready track in Owosso on January 12, 1980. [*Top photo, author's collection; bottom photo by Dennis Schmidt*]

LOCOMOTIVE TRANSITIONS: In May 1981, eleven months before the Ann Arbor car ferries ceased operations, Michigan Interstate #391 and #390 (above) prepare to take a train out of Toledo. These engines—and eight other GP35s from the AA roster—were later transferred to the Tuscola & Saginaw Bay, which began serving the line from Ann Arbor to Alma in October 1982 as Michigan Interstate transitioned into a shortline. Below, Michigan Interstate #7, an Alco S3 switching locomotive built for the AA in 1950, wastes its compelling new paint job as it rusts away in an Owosso deadline in October 1983. [*Photographers unknown; author's collection*]

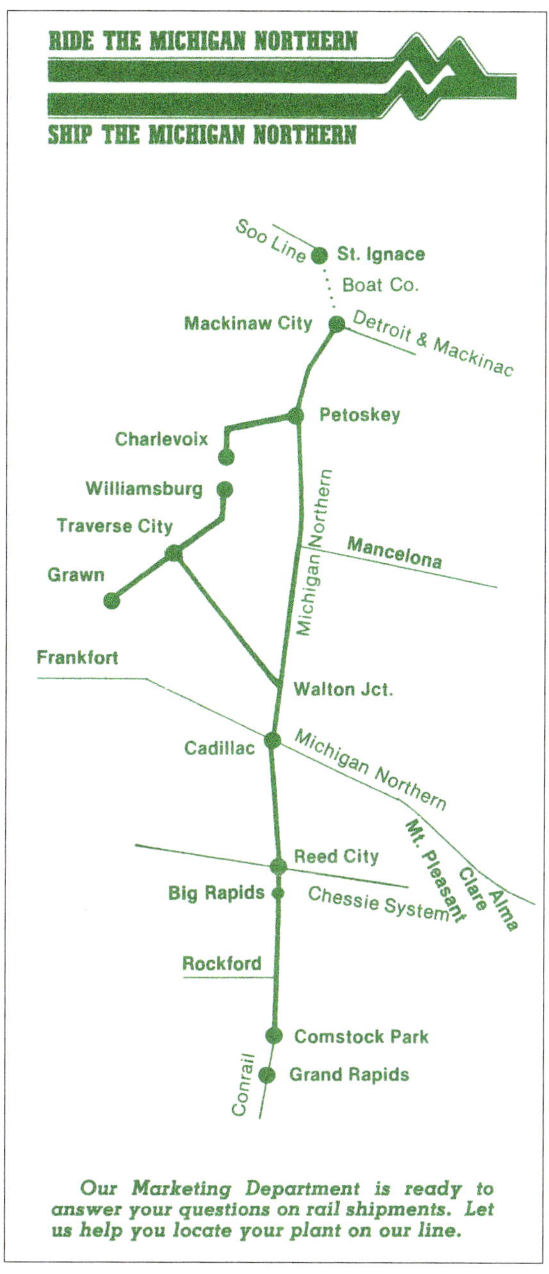

SHIP THE MICHIGAN NORTHERN: A 1983 system map showed the Michigan Northern Railway at its brief peak. In October 1982, in addition to its core 220-mile Mackinaw City to Comstock Park (Grand Rapids) line, the MN began handling traffic on the Alma to Frankfort portion of the Ann Arbor, another 146 miles. The shortline worked the Alma-Frankfort line only until May 1984, but served shippers elsewhere in the state for more than a decade, from its creation in 1976 during the Conrail reconfiguration until the end finally came in 1987. [*Author's collection*]

NEW IN TOWN: When state officials designated Michigan Northern as operator of the former Ann Arbor line between Alma and Elberta-Frankfort in 1982, business on the segment was based out of Cadillac. In September 1983, a crew working with GP7 #1603 is taking care of the day's switching duties at Alma. At AA milepost 145.8, Alma is almost exactly halfway between Toledo and Elberta. [*Photo by Dennis Schmidt*]

UPBEAT APPROACH: Headquartered in Cadillac, Michigan Northern presented a professional and aggressive "can do" attitude, as this sign outside the shortline's office building in May 1982 attests. [*Photo by Dennis Schmidt*]

THE CHIEF: Michigan Northern billed itself as the "Mackinaw Gateway Route" for good reason. The shortline interchanged with the car ferry *Chief Wawatam*, which moved freight cars between Mackinaw City, at the northern tip of Michigan's Lower Peninsula, and St. Ignace, in the Upper Peninsula directly across the Straits of Mackinac. *Chief Wawatam*, featured in this postcard, was launched in 1911. Ferry service here ended in August 1984. [*Author's collection*]

UPPER PENINSULA TRANSFER: Soo Line Railroad's 28-mile branch from Trout Lake to St. Ignace provided access to traffic carried across the Straits of Mackinac on the *Chief Wawatam*. On October 8, 1981, Soo #4406 is in St. Ignace with a long line of boxcars and a Seaboard passenger car. Once car ferry operations halted, Soo Line soon axed the branch, abandoning it in 1986. [*Photo by Dennis Schmidt*]

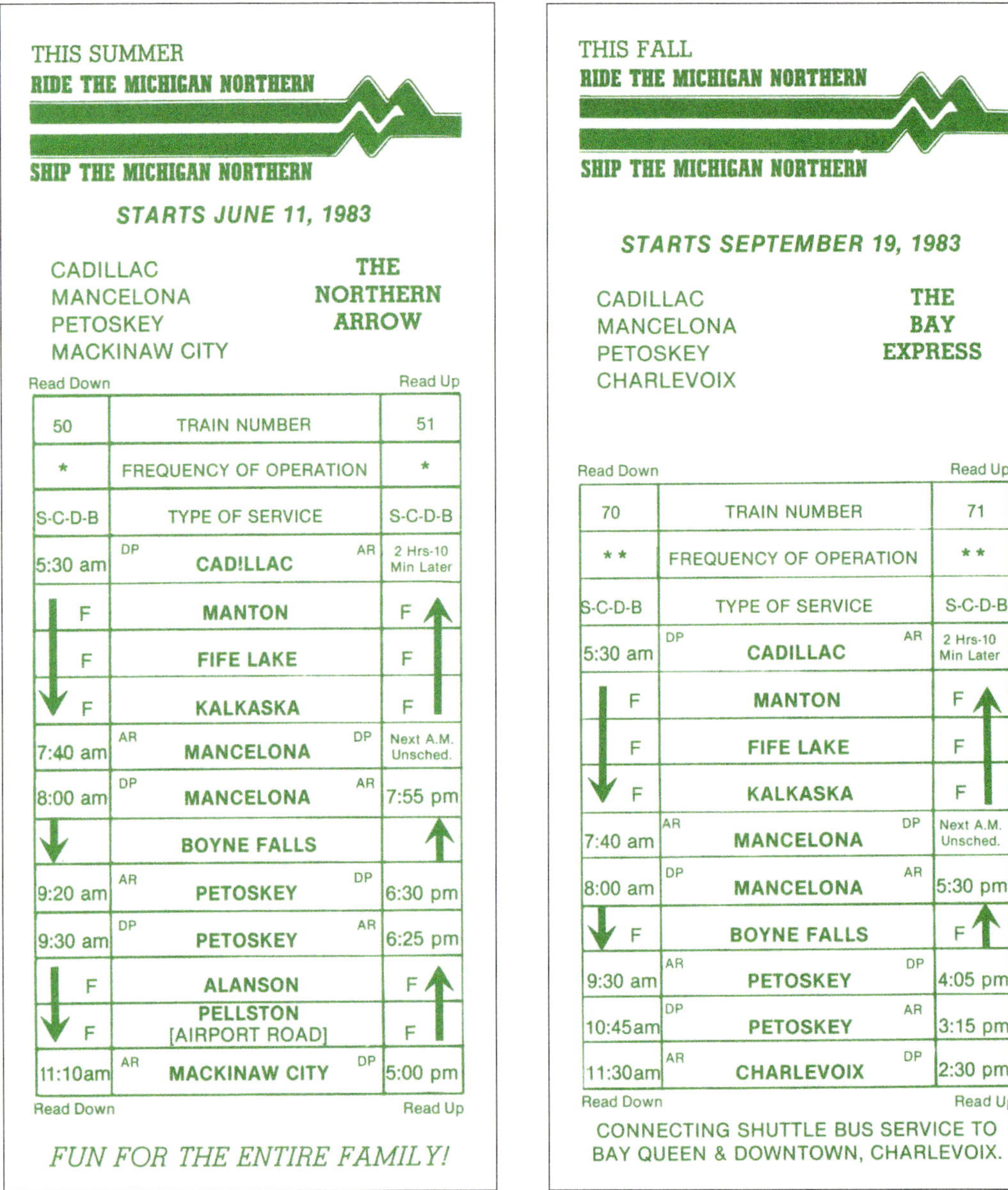

Read Down			Read Up
50	TRAIN NUMBER		51
*	FREQUENCY OF OPERATION		*
S-C-D-B	TYPE OF SERVICE		S-C-D-B
5:30 am DP	CADILLAC	AR	2 Hrs-10 Min Later
F	MANTON		F
F	FIFE LAKE		F
F	KALKASKA		F
7:40 am AR	MANCELONA	DP	Next A.M. Unsched.
8:00 am DP	MANCELONA	AR	7:55 pm
	BOYNE FALLS		
9:20 am AR	PETOSKEY	DP	6:30 pm
9:30 am DP	PETOSKEY	AR	6:25 pm
F	ALANSON		F
F	PELLSTON [AIRPORT ROAD]		F
11:10am AR	MACKINAW CITY	DP	5:00 pm

Read Down			Read Up
70	TRAIN NUMBER		71
**	FREQUENCY OF OPERATION		**
S-C-D-B	TYPE OF SERVICE		S-C-D-B
5:30 am DP	CADILLAC	AR	2 Hrs-10 Min Later
F	MANTON		F
F	FIFE LAKE		F
F	KALKASKA		F
7:40 am AR	MANCELONA	DP	Next A.M. Unsched.
8:00 am DP	MANCELONA	AR	5:30 pm
F	BOYNE FALLS		F
9:30 am AR	PETOSKEY	DP	4:05 pm
10:45am DP	PETOSKEY	AR	3:15 pm
11:30am AR	CHARLEVOIX	DP	2:30 pm

NORTHERN ARROW AND BAY EXPRESS: In 1983, Michigan Northern promoted passenger excursion service in an effort to boost the shortline's increasingly meager revenue stream. The *Northern Arrow* traveled between Cadillac and Mackinaw City via Petoskey, while the *Bay Express* made trips between Cadillac and Charlevoix. The tourist-oriented trains lasted only two seasons. [*Author's collection*]

SNOW SWITCH: Colorful Toledo, Peoria & Western GP7 #103 switches freight cars in the snow at Alma on January 17, 1984, while on the Michigan Northern roster. Less than four months later, the Michigan Department of Transportation displaced Michigan Northern and designated a new railroad—the Tuscola & Saginaw Bay, which was already covering the 102 miles between Ann Arbor and Alma—to also take over freight operations from Alma to Frankfort, another 146 miles. [*Photo by Dennis Schmidt*]

NEW PLAYER: Until it began serving segments of the former Ann Arbor in 1982, the Tuscola & Saginaw Bay was an obscure 44-mile shortline created in 1977 out of Penn Central trackage in Michigan's "thumb" area. In February 1980, #4946, a covered hopper built in May 1979, shows off its bold lettering in the snow at the railroad's home base in Vassar, Michigan. [*Photo by Dennis Schmidt*]

CADILLAC BLACK: Two T&SB locomotives are ready to pull a train south out of Cadillac in September 1991. Heading out are #394, named *City of Clare*, and #392, which remains in Ann Arbor paint, but with its former identity with predecessor Michigan Interstate unceremoniously blacked out. [*Photographer unknown; author's collection*]

WAITING FOR THE SNOW: As the winter season nears in 1992, a seemingly forgotten snowplow rests among autumn weeds on a storage track adjacent to the former Ann Arbor mainline at Durand, Michigan.

NORTHBOUND AT ALMA: A T&SB freight is headed through the snowy cold at Alma on March 10, 1999, with two ex-Ann Arbor engines handling the work. [*Photo by Dennis Schmidt*]

FIFTY YEARS AT CLARE: The railroad infrastructure evolved dramatically at Clare in the latter part of the twentieth century. In the 1953 scene above, an Ann Arbor "FT" freight crosses the Chesapeake & Ohio mainline as the station agent hoops up orders to the crew. Fifty-two years later, in 2005, the view from the same vantage point (below) is vastly different: The semaphore signals, interlocking tower, and C&O's east-west route between Saginaw and Ludington are all long gone, while the ex-AA tracks host freight activity on a significantly reduced scale. [*Top photo author's collection*]

LIGHTS OUT: The Ann Arbor crossed C&O's Saginaw-Ludington mainline at Clare, AA milepost 178.8, and it was an active interchange station until the C&O abandoned the route in 1987. In this autumn 1992 scene looking east, the C&O line has been torn up and the signal tower that once protected the crossing with the AA no longer has any purpose; its lights have been turned off and away.

NEW CUSTOMER IN CLARE: Big changes are obvious in these two scenes looking west from where the C&O and Ann Arbor tracks intersected at Clare. In the top photo, taken in 1992, the ex-C&O mainline that once went all the way to Ludington on the Lake Michigan shoreline trails off to nowhere in the wake of the route being abandoned in 1987. In the same view from 2005 (below), a company called Northern Dry Bulk has rebuilt a short stretch of the old C&O right of way into a major shipping facility that brings in carloads of plastic resin by rail.

MESICK LOOKING SOUTH: The Ann Arbor mainline at Mesick (milepost 254.1) is obscured by weeds and grass in a scene captured on June 28, 1999—closing in on two decades since daily freight trains stopped passing through on their way to and from Elberta. Faintly visible to the right of the main track is a short siding the railroad's 1964 timetable shows as having a capacity of twenty-eight 50-foot freight cars.

CROSSBUCKS: Although the rails here had long been out of service, these crossbucks—with their fading Ann Arbor heritage still plainly visible in August 1997—silently protect a rural road crossing in Thompsonville. At this time, the tracks through this small Michigan community at AA milepost 270.3 had not seen regular freight train traffic for about fifteen years.

DISCONNECT: Thompsonville's landmark water reservoir looms over the landscape in these scenes from October 1992. The obsolete interchange track, where the Ann Arbor and the Chesapeake & Ohio once swapped freight cars to expedite transit times for their customers, switches off from the AA mainline into oblivion. The antique switch stand remains, but by this time the AA tracks were out of service, while the C&O line—which ran between Manistee and Traverse City—is gone, leaving only the diamond where the two rail lines intersected.

PENN CENTRAL
5666
5666

WOODARD FURNITURE COMPANY
GREAT LAKES CENTRAL
385
385
GLC
Railroad

POWER MOVE: Several Great Lakes Central engines tie up traffic in downtown Owosso as they head out in July 2014. The locomotives will soon cut north onto the ex-Penn Central Saginaw Branch, which originated in Jackson and went to Saginaw and Bay City via Lansing and Owosso. The branch now ends twenty miles north of Owosso in Fergus, while to the south, Owosso to Lansing has been abandoned.

OPPOSITE PAGE:

CHANGING SEASONS: Colors change to reflect the transition in the Owosso area over several decades. Above, on a wintry December day in 1969, black Penn Central GP7 #5666 idles next to the local freight house. Some forty years later, in November 2009, Great Lakes Central GP35 #385 (below) is parked on former Ann Arbor tracks in Owosso's warehouse district. GLC took over the route from Ann Arbor to Yuma in 2006. [*Both photos by Dennis Schmidt*]

TO THE DISTANCE: In the 1970s, this would have been the view looking west along the mainline of Grand Trunk Western's Grand Rapids Subdivision (above), and the track switching off to the right would have led into the Ann Arbor's Owosso yard complex (below). Yet seen here in June 2006, the former GTW mainline is used only for yard moves and to access a shipper, the tracks beyond Owosso to Grand Rapids are gone, and Great Lakes Central is running the show in the freight yard.

EXCESS TANKS (LEFT): Stored tank cars fill the siding at Cohoctah, Michigan, in the summer of 2014. This station on the old AA mainline is now served by Great Lakes Central.

CROSSING GUARD (RIGHT): Weathered and aging signal lights protect the CSX/Great Lakes Central crossing at Ann Pere, Michigan. Ann Pere is located roughly halfway between Ann Arbor and Owosso.

ANN ARBOR/PERE MARQUETTE: CSX SD40-3 #4011 rolls over the ex-Ann Arbor main at Ann Pere as the crew prepares to collect cars at the junction in July 2014 (above). Ann Pere, at AA milepost 72.0, was named for the original two railroads that intersected here—Ann Arbor and Pere Marquette. The location is still busy, although now it is Great Lakes Central and CSX, respectively, interchanging cars here. Below, the author revels in exploring Ann Pere. [*Bottom photo by Larry Moon Yaek*]

SWAP MEET: Freight cars await pickup from the Ann Pere interchange tracks as Great Lakes Central's rails (top photo) cut across the CSX diamond in this view looking south along the former Ann Arbor mainline. With red signals protecting the crossing with the GLC (bottom photo), the CSX route between Grand Rapids and Detroit leads southeast from Ann Pere as it heads toward Detroit.

COMMUTER VISIONS: In August 2014, Great Lakes Central, the Michigan Department of Transportation, and Owosso-based Steam Railroading Institute banded together to provide a series of passenger excursions between Howell and Cohoctah. The rides were designed to promote proposed commuter rail service between Ann Arbor and Howell. [*Photo by Drayton Blackgrove*]

GOOD NEIGHBORS: Canadian National #2612 switches cars in the former Grand Trunk Western yard in Durand in July 2014. The Ann Arbor once rode its own mainline between Durand and Owosso, but since GTW ran a parallel route between the two towns, the AA obtained trackage rights on the GTW line in the mid-1970s, allowing it to abandon approximately ten miles of redundant track.

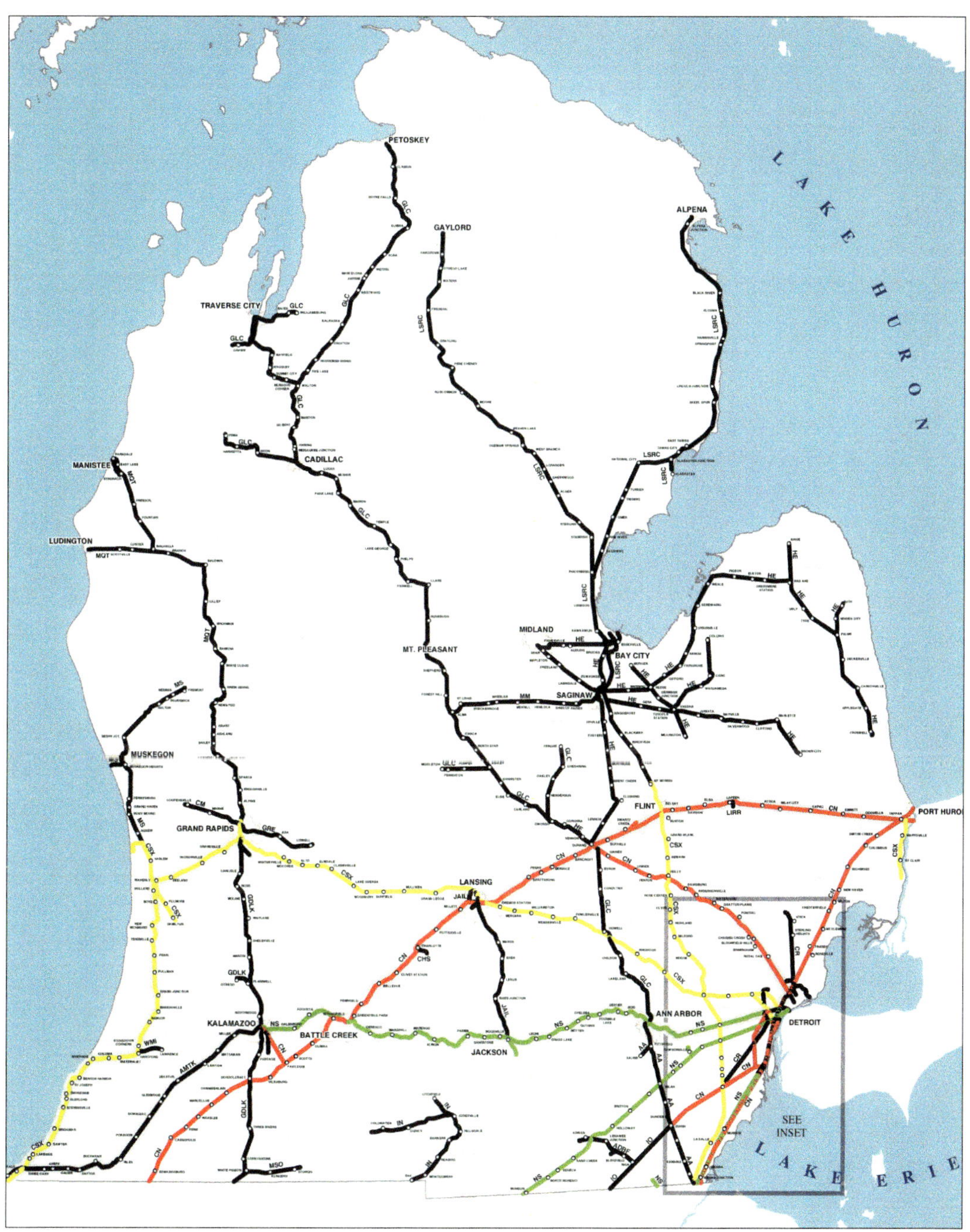

RAIL NETWORK: Rail lines in the Lower Peninsula of Michigan are shown in this color-coded Department of Transportation map from 2017. Ann Arbor Railroad trackage between Toledo and Ann Arbor is shown in black and designated "AA," while Great Lakes Central—which handles the old AA mainline from Ann Arbor to Yuma—is also in black, with "GLC" designating its extensive routes. [*Courtesy of Michigan Department of Transportation*]

ROLLING MUSEUM: The Steam Railroading Institute, founded for the preservation, restoration, and operation of historical railroad equipment, created a standing exhibit of freight cars in Owosso to capture some of the history of Michigan's transportation landscape. Highlights on display in July 2011 included AA caboose #2839, in its Wabash-era paint; a Wabash boxcar; and a Pere Marquette double-door boxcar (below) designed to carry furniture or automobiles.

4

THE AA'S GP35 FLEET DISPERSES

The C&O's once-busy Boardman Yard was desolate. A key line of the Pennsylvania Railroad used to come in nearby, meeting with the C&O at an obscure crossing near the southeastern edge of Traverse City. A crewman had to leave the train to unlock and swing aside a heavy iron gate protecting the C&O's main track. They were called "smash boards." If your train smashed into one, you were in big trouble.

D. C. Jesse Burkhardt, journal entry, June 25, 1976

SOUTH OF PETOSKEY: Great Lakes Central #394 and #395 are pulling a five-car train south on the regional carrier's line between Petoskey and Cadillac in July 2017. Repainting into GLC colors has not yet happened for GP35 #394, an ex-Tuscola & Saginaw Bay unit (and ex-Ann Arbor before that) that badly needs a fresh coat of paint.

71

MORE ROOM TO ROAM: With the demise of the Ann Arbor, the railroad's GP35s were moved to parts of Michigan they'd never experienced before. One line that began hosting the Annie's locomotives was Penn Central's Grand Rapids to Mackinaw City route, a section of which is seen here (top) looking south from snowy Walton Junction. Below, ex-Ann Arbor #390—under the ownership of Tuscola & Saginaw Bay and with its once-proud Ann Arbor lettering painted over—is faithfully working the line in October 1992, pulling three cars south through Manton on the way to Cadillac.

WEST OF THE AA LINE: T&SB #385 and #390 head a grain train being loaded on former Grand Trunk Western rails at Middleton, Michigan, in March 2000. These two engines were among the ten factory-new GP35s—road numbers #385-#394—the Ann Arbor took delivery of in 1964, the year after DT&I purchased the railroad. As of 2020, four of the ten had been scrapped (#386, #387, #388, #389), three were still in regular use by Great Lakes Central (#390, #392, #393), and three (#385, #391, #394) remained on the GLC roster with their fate uncertain. [*Photo by Dennis Schmidt*]

BEER RUN: A GP35 pulls a lone boxcar on a long stretch of straight track near Acme, Michigan, in October 1994. The branch line was formed out of ex-C&O tracks between Traverse City and Williamsburg, where a beer distributor is located. Before abandonments in 1982, the rails continued another seventy miles north from Williamsburg to Petoskey and Bay View. [*Photographer unknown; author's collection*]

SPECIAL DELIVERY: T&SB's ex-AA #393, *City of Cadillac,* bakes in the sun after delivering an oversized and overweight electrical transformer to a Consumer's Power substation outside Traverse City on July 15, 2002. The move required the use of a specialized six-axle flatcar with a depressed center section. Since the 1960s, the 26-mile former Pennsylvania Railroad branch line from Walton Junction into Traverse City has been operated by Penn Central, Michigan Northern, Tuscola & Saginaw Bay, and Great Lakes Central.

CHANGE OF SCENERY: One of the few remaining GP35s from the Ann Arbor roster, Tuscola & Saginaw Bay #390 hustles north with a few loads bound for Traverse City in July 2002. [*Photo by Linda Norris*]

BOARDMAN YARD: Once an active facility, the former C&O/Chessie System terminal in Traverse City, known as Boardman Yard (top photo) was in rapid decline by the 1980s. In this 1999 view, the engine house in the background stood empty and freight movements were "as needed." From Boardman, trains go southwest only as far as Grawn or northeast to Williamsburg. Below, T&SB #388 passes the former Pere Marquette/C&O depot in Traverse City on its way to Williamsburg in October 1992. [*Bottom photo author's collection*]

BLUE POWER: GLC #385, a former AA unit, leads three other GLC engines into Oakley, Michigan, on the castoff Penn Central line between Owosso and Saginaw. The Ann Arbor "inherited" most of the branch when Conrail was created in 1976. The locomotives are on their way to Oakley's grain elevators, where they will hook on to a long line of hoppers ready to be hauled south to Toledo.

WON'T RUN HERE: Ann Arbor GP35s will never experience this portion of the C&O's east-west route between Saginaw and Ludington. The rails west of Clare, seen here in 2005 vanishing under lush vegetation, were abandoned as far as Baldwin, roughly 57 miles, in 1987. Also removed was the 31-mile segment that went east from Clare to Midland. The Clare-Midland mileage has been transformed into the Pere Marquette Rail-Trail.

5

SHORTLINE SURVIVOR:
ANN ARBOR TO TOLEDO

From Ann Arbor late at night. I was showing Moon the ropes, as by now I was feeling the oats of my experience. We rode south on the "Annie" to Diann, Michigan, where the Detroit, Toledo & Ironton crossed the Ann Arbor line. We left the AA there, and waited for a DT&I westbound. A DT&I freight came in early in the morning and stopped to work the junction.

D. C. Jesse Burkhardt, journal entry, October 5, 1973

HOME BASE: The Ann Arbor Railroad's operational headquarters is Ottawa Yard in Toledo, Ohio, seen here on a stormy June 18, 2017. The shortline moves freight between Toledo and just north of Ann Arbor, Michigan, about 50 miles. [*Photo by Peter Hayes*]

PENN CENTRAL VINTAGE: Ann Arbor GP38 #7791, previously on the Conrail roster, waits on a service track at Toledo in June 2003. The shortline obtained a total of three ex-Conrail GP38s in the mid-1980s; #7771 and #7802 were the other two road numbers. All three locomotives were built for Penn Central in 1969. [*Photographer unknown; author's collection*]

HURON RIVER CROSSING: Captured from a drone, Ann Arbor units #4049 and #2373 haul seven hoppers southward on the railroad's picturesque bridge over the Huron River in Ann Arbor on April 9, 2020. [*Photo by Ryan Katon*]

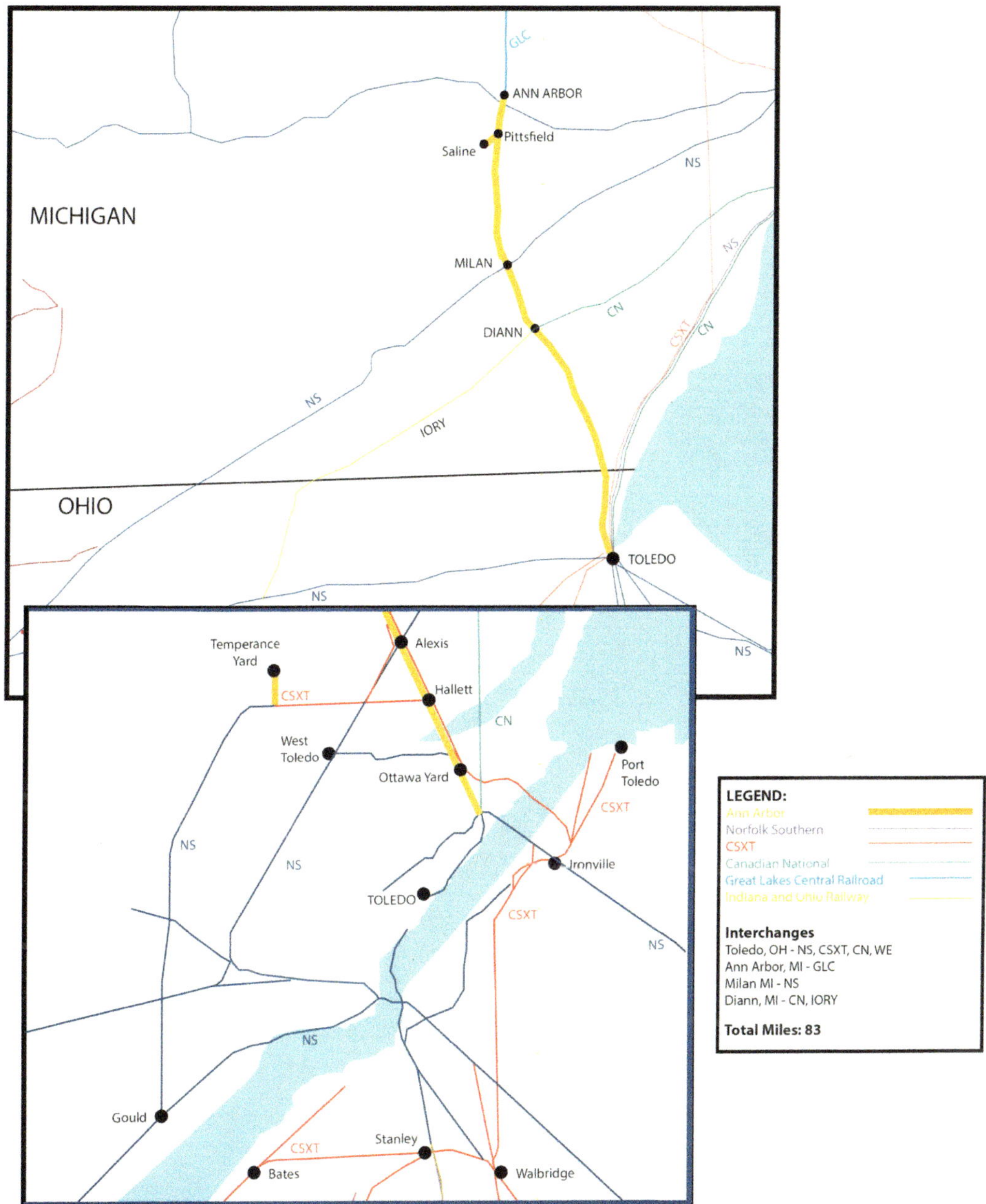

DOUBLE A STILL ROLLING: A map of the Ann Arbor Railroad displays the shortline as it exists in 2020, with an inset map showing its operational territory in Toledo. The "modern" AA took root in 1977 out of what was previously the Michigan Interstate Railway Company, the designated operator the state of Michigan put in place to move freight along the original Ann Arbor's entire Toledo-Frankfort route. Long story short, a legal dispute with the state in 1982 led Michigan Interstate to retreat to just the Toledo to Ann Arbor segment. After reorganization and ownership changes, the shortline still stands. [*Author's collection*]

DIANN STRAIGHT: The Ann Arbor's mainline heads south out of Diann, Michigan, in an unusually straight line on its way toward Toledo, as seen here in 2005. The east-west tracks crossing the AA in the foreground basically mark where operations along this former Detroit, Toledo & Ironton route are now divided between two railroads that have taken over: transcontinental carrier Canadian National moves traffic east of Diann, while shortline Indiana & Ohio Railroad operates west of Diann.

BOARDED UP: Diann, at milepost 20.5 on the Ann Arbor line, was once a key interchange point for the AA and the DT&I. But when this westward-looking photograph of the crossing and the closed interlocking tower was taken in April 2005, the interchange tracks behind the building stood empty and rusting, and the DT&I was just a memory.

PITTSFIELD CROSSING: Signal towers on AA rails at Pittsfield Junction, Michigan, protect the crossing of what used to be a New York Central line that went from Ypsilanti, Michigan, to Fort Wayne, Indiana. Most of the NYC route was abandoned in the 1960s, but a 5-mile segment between Saline and Pittsfield remained to access a Ford auto parts plant in Saline. The Ann Arbor gained access to the branch in 1968.

APRIL SNOW: A late season snowfall dusts the AA mainline at Pittsfield, at milepost 40.4, in April 2005. The AA's Saline Branch crosses the main here as it cuts west toward Saline.

TRADING TRAINS: After delivering a long cut of grain hoppers to the Great Lakes Central at the Osmer interchange yard north of Ann Arbor on October 19, 2018 (above), the three Ann Arbor locomotives that hauled the train up from Toledo—#3927, #3904, and #1337—wait as the GLC crew prepares to take the cars north. Below, the AA train is headed back to Toledo after exchanging cars with GLC. [*Both photos by Peter Hayes*]

SALINE BRANCH ACTION: After switching the Visteon auto parts plant on the Saline Branch, an Ann Arbor local pulls a string of excess-height boxcars east toward Pittsfield Junction. When this scene was captured in March 2005, Visteon, a Ford spinoff, required rail service five days a week. In 2020, the branch line is used for storage only because Faurecia, the company currently operating the plant, no longer moves its products by rail. [*Photo by Kristian Foondle*]

NOT THE ONLY RAILROAD IN TOWN: Although the Ann Arbor Railroad was named after the city, the more active line through Ann Arbor is Norfolk Southern's ex-New York Central route that links Detroit and Chicago and hosts daily passenger trains. In June 2006, Amtrak's eastbound *Wolverine* is stopped next to the city's historic Michigan Central railroad depot, which has been converted into a classy restaurant called the Gandy Dancer.

END OF TRACK: A battered double-door boxcar with the "ferry in the fog" logo, from the years the railroad operated as the Michigan Interstate/Ann Arbor Railroad System, stands alone at the western end of the Saline Branch in November 2013. A fading black stencil (below) calls for the car to be returned to Saline "when empty," but the boxcar is no longer in revenue service; it is used only to store tools and maintenance equipment.

WABASH HERITAGE: The Ann Arbor cuts across the double-track mainlines of Norfolk Southern at Milan, Michigan, at AA milepost 30.8. Before it was Norfolk Southern, the railroad that connected with the Ann Arbor here was known as Norfolk & Western, and before that it was the Wabash Railroad, the AA's parent company from 1925 until 1963. The Wabash was merged into Norfolk & Western in 1964.

ACTIVE INTERCHANGE: Thirty miles north of the railroad's home terminal at Toledo, Ann Arbor GP39-2s #2368 and #2373—both previously Union Pacific units still in the distinctive UP colors—work the Norfolk Southern/AA interchange tracks at Milan.

JEEP PATROL: In a "heritage" paint scheme honoring the company's origins, Ann Arbor GP38 #3879 switches auto-carriers in a yard serving a Jeep assembly plant in Toledo on August 5, 2015. [*Photo by Drayton Blackgrove*]

MINT CONDITION: Ann Arbor #3879 is briefly dormant alongside yard tracks packed with freight cars in Toledo's Ottawa Yard on September 29, 2015. The immaculate locomotive, in pristine paint and basking in the soft lighting of an Ohio sunrise, almost seems to be posing for a portrait. [*Photo by Peter Hayes*]

6

PATH THROUGH HISTORY:
THE BETSIE VALLEY TRAIL

I walked to the Ann Arbor freight yard in Elberta—Boat Landing Yard—but there was nothing going on. No switching and no strings ready to roll. The economy, it seemed, had passed northern Michigan by; there was little freight to be hauled.

D. C. Jesse Burkhardt, journal entry, July 7, 1979

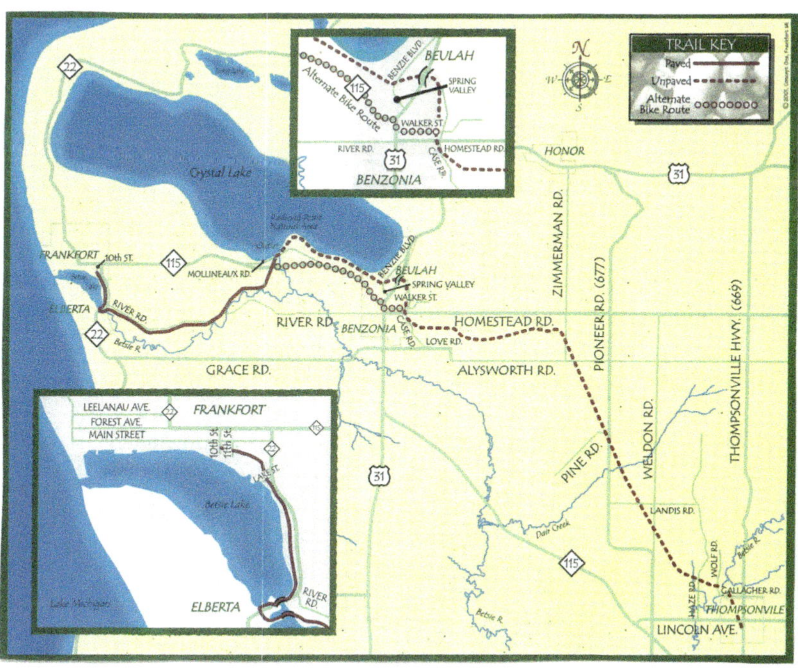

SCENIC CORRIDOR: The Betsie Valley Trail follows the abandoned mainline of the Ann Arbor Railroad between Elberta-Frankfort and Thompsonville, approximately twenty-two miles. The trail opened to the public in 2005. [*Map courtesy of Friends of the Betsie Valley Trail*]

91

EVOLUTION: Its rails stripped away, what remains of a bridge across a section of the Betsie River just outside Elberta in July 2002 marks the now-silent route of the Ann Arbor. After the mid-1980s, with trains no longer running, Friends of the Betsie Valley Trail helped repurpose the almost forgotten bridge into part of a scenic trail.

WILDLIFE WARNING: In the summer months, turtles, snakes, frogs, and other wild creatures are commonly encountered along the old right of way, especially on the 10-mile stretch between Frankfort and Beulah. A creative sign outside Frankfort alerts bicyclists to be careful not to run over any animals.

CROWDED LOGS: Colorful and wary painted turtles bask in the summer sunshine alongside the Betsie Valley Trail. Portions of the recreational corridor parallel the Betsie River, and turtles are often seen. The painted turtle was designated as Michigan's state reptile in 1995.

CRYSTAL LAKE ROUTE:
A few miles out of Frankfort, the rail trail runs directly beside beautiful Crystal Lake (top), a scenic highlight of the pathway. Below: The first 6.7 miles of the former mainline roadbed are paved, and the flat grade allows for fast biking, so "15 mph" speed limit signs are displayed.

RIDE TO BEULAH: The author at the rebuilt Ann Arbor Railroad depot in Beulah, Michigan, in June 2017, after a day on the Betsie Valley Trail. [*Photo by Renae Cannon*]

THOMPSONVILLE TRIBUTE: The rail trail extends twenty-two miles from Frankfort to rural Thompsonville. Near the end of the route in Thompsonville is this ex-Burlington Northern caboose. It was donated to the community as a tribute to the importance of the two railroads, Ann Arbor and Pere Marquette, that intersected here and helped build the town. [*Photo by Tom Lacinski*]

SLASHING WAVES (LEFT): This artistic and dramatic postcard, designed by Lantern Press in Seattle, Washington, depicts the lighthouse at the end of the Frankfort Harbor breakwater. Past this lighthouse, countless car ferries came and went during the ninety years the Ann Arbor's big boats sailed. [*Author's collection*]

COFFEE CONNECTION (RIGHT): The spirit of the "Annie" continues to live on through mementos such as this logo-emblazoned coffee mug. The logo's design was often described as "ferry in the fog," sparking AA devotee Eric Wagner to comment cleverly that drinking coffee from the cup "clears the morning fog." [*Photo by Tom Lacinski*]